Hammer Horror Trivia

Alan Toner

Copyright © 2017 Alan Toner
All rights reserved.

ISBN-13: 978-1976084041
ISBN-10: 1976084040

Other Books By Alan Toner

Famous Psychics
Hammer Horror Remembered
100 True Ghost Stories
100 True Ghost Stories Vol. 2
Haunted Objects
True Ghost Stories
True Ghost Stories 2
True Ghost Stories 3
True Ghost Stories 4
UK UFOs
Werewolf Nightmare
Horror Stories
Horror Stories 2

Contents

1. General Hammer Studio Facts..........................1
2. The Dracula Films..........................7
3. The Frankenstein Films..........................14
4. Werewolves, Reptiles and Zombies..........................20
5. The Mummy Films..........................23
6. The Quatermass Films..........................27
7. The Swashbuckling Films..........................33
 8. The Karnstein Trilogy..........................36
9. Rasputin The Mad Monk..........................40
10. The Prehistoric Films..........................42
11. The Hands of the Ripper..........................47
 12. The Anniversary and The Nanny..........................49
13. Hammer House of Horror TV Series..........................52
14. The She Films..........................54
15. The Abominable Snowman..........................56
16. Countess Dracula..........................57
17. The Hound of the Baskervilles..........................59
18. The Devil Rides Out..........................62
19. The Journey To The Unknown TV Series..........................64
20. Dr Jekyll and Sister Hyde..........................66
21. To The Devil A Daughter..........................67
22. Vampire Circus..........................70
23. The Legend of the Seven Golden Vampires..........................72
24. The Woman in Black..........................74
25. The Quiet Ones..........................76
26. Let Me In..........................77
27. Wake Wood..........................79

28. The Resident...81
Author's Note..82

1. General Hammer Studio Facts

Hammer Film Productions was founded in November 1934. Its founders were James Carreras, Enrique Carrearas and William Hinds. It is one of the oldest film studios in the world.

It may come as a surprise to some Hammer fans, but the studio's horror movies made up only one third of its total output. The company involved itself in other genres like psychological thrillers, sci fi (the Quatermass movies being the notable example of this), swashbuckling films and noir.

Before World War II, Hammer's 5-movie output was predominantly comedy (*The Public Life of Henry the Ninth*) and slave drama (The Song of Freedom). They also got Bela Lugosi for an appearance in the movie *The Mystery of The Marie Celeste.*

Once World War II broke out, production at Hammer was ceased, as its executives were enlisted in active service.

Hammer's very first movie was *The Public Life of Henry the Ninth* (1935).

Alan Toner

Hammer Studios went into liquidation amid a slump in the British film industry in 1937. However, Exclusive survived, and on the 20th July 1937 purchased the leasehold on 113-117 Wardour Street. They continued to distribute films for other companies.

When the Second World War ended, Hammer was re-formed, amid a growing demand for more British-produced supporting movies, and began to produce crime movies and boy's own adventure stories.

In the 1950s Hammer started to produce a series of support drama and documentaries, both of which were to run alongside feature films in the cinema.

In 1951 Hammer started to develop its North American market by co-producing movies with American producer Robert Lippert. These American movies were mostly crime thrillers such as *Bad Blonde*, *Man Bait* and *Terror Street*.

In 1954 Hammer made its first colour feature film: *The Men of Sherwood Forest*. This movie marked Hammer's return to adventure stories.

The year 1955 marked a significant moment in Hammer history, for that was the year when it produced *The Quatermass Experiment*. This movie was a big commercial success for the studio, and attracted much critical acclaim.

Appreciating the success of *The Quatermass Experiment*, Hammer moved away from the financially unrewarding crime thrillers and began focus on horror.

The Hammer Horror Fact Book

The Curse of Frankenstein (1957) marked the beginning of Hammer's legendary excursion into the horror genre. Starring Christopher Lee as the monster and Peter Cushing as the evil Baron, is was the studio's first full-colour horror movie.

Spurred on by the huge box office success of *The Curse of Frankenstein*, Hammer wasted no time in following up that movie by revisiting another classic monster for the big screen, this time *Dracula* (1958). The evil count was played brilliantly by Christopher Lee, and again Peter Cushing starred alongside him, this time in the good guy role as the vampire hunter Van Helsing. The movie was released under the title *Horror of Dracula* in America. Just like *Curse of Frankenstein*, Dracula was another big box office success for the studio, and made household names of Christopher Lee and Peter Cushing. These two movies alone carved an important, much-revered place for Hammer in horror movie history.

Revelling in the tremendous successes of both *Curse of Frankenstein* and *Dracula*, Hammer went on to make two more monster movies in the late fifties: *The Abominable Snowman* (1957) and *The Mummy* (1959).

Oakley Court is a Victorian Gothic country house set in 35 acres overlooking the River Thames in the parish of Bray, Berkshire. In August 1949, Hammer started using the house as a film production studio. They shot five films there before relocating to the nearby Down Place - which later became Bray Studios - the following year.

Alan Toner

Whilst the vast majority of Hammer's horror movies were filmed at Bray in the late 50s and early 60s, the studio occasionally used Oakley Court as an exterior location, for example in *The Brides of Dracula* (1962), *The Reptile* (1966) and *The Plague of the Zombies* (1966).

In 1967 Hammer left Bray Studios for Elstree.

The average Hammer horror movie cost less than £100,000 to make in those days.

Hammer used the same studio sets for both *Dracula* (1958) and *The Revenge of Frankenstein* (1958). The only difference was that they just swapped the furniture around.

Not a lot of people know that Peter Sellers actually starred in a Hammer film. He played a naval officer in the 1968 comedy *Up The Creek*.

Hammer used legendary actor Oliver Reed quite often in their early 1960s movies. His most famous performance was in *Curse of the Werewolf* (1961), which was Hammer's only excursion into the werewolf genre.

In 1968, whilst making *Dracula Has Risen From The Grave* on the set of Pinewood Studios, Hammer was presented with the 1968 Queen Elizabeth Award for Industry in recognition of their remarkable success in raising money for Britain.

Although Hammer enjoyed a remarkable popularity with

their aesthetically-appealing Gothic horror films from the 1950s to the early 70s, significant changes in the genre, with the release of more contemporary shockers like *Rosemary's Baby* (1968) and *The Exorcist* (1973), made the B-movie productions of Hammer start to look slightly dated and tame, especially to American viewers. Consequently, whilst Hammer did continue to produce their signature horror movies right through to the mid-seventies in the face of the competition presented by these new shocker movies, the studio had lost much of its appeal.

Much to the delight of the die-hard Hammer fans, the studio has begun to make something of a comeback, albeit in a different form. Although dabbling in various film projects, it is still predominantly geared towards the horror genre.

New Hammer's most popular release to date has been *The Woman In Black* (2012) starring Daniel Radcliffe.

In October 1978, singer Kate Bush released a song, which was kind of nod to the Hammer films, called (appropriately enough) *Hammer Horror*.

In 2015 Hammer released a follow-up to *The Woman In Black* called *The Woman In Black 2: Angel of Death*. Set some 40 years after the events of the first movie, this sequel was not as critically acclaimed as its elegant, spine-chilling predecessor, suffering from a lack of pace and excessive dialogue.

In 2014 Hammer touched on the poltergeist theme with *The Quiet Ones*. Starring Jared Harris as a university professor attempting to prove poltergeists (or the so-called "noisy ghosts") are nothing more than manifestations of the human psyche, as opposed to actual supernatural entities, the movie was described by one critic as "trading too heavily on past glories."

In 2010 Hammer acquired the English rights to the Swedish vampire film *Let The Right One In* and produced *Let Me In*. The writer and director Mike Reeves made several changes to the British version of the movie, like relocating the setting from Stockholm to New Mexico and renaming the lead characters. Let Me In received great critical acclaim upon its release.

In 2008 Hammer shot an Irish horror movie called *Wake Wood*. This was filmed partly in County Donegal and partly in Scania, Sweden. Starring Timothy Spall and in the tradition of *The Wicker Man* and *Don't Look Now*, *Wake Wood* dealt with the subject of gruesome rituals and resurrected corpses.

In 2011 long-time Hammer stalwart Christopher Lee returned for a cameo appearance in *The Resident*. Also starring Hilary Swank, the movie told the story of a recently single woman who rents an apartment in New York City and comes to believe that somebody is stalking her.

2. The Dracula Films

Christopher Lee played Count Dracula in a total of 7 films for Hammer: *Dracula* (1958), *Dracula Prince of Darkness* (1966), *Dracula Has Risen From The Grave* (1968), *Taste The Blood of Dracula* (1970), *Scars of Dracula* (1970), *Dracula AD 1972* (1972) and *The Satanic Rites of Dracula* (1973).

The only two Dracula-titled Hammer films that did not feature Christopher Lee were *The Brides of Dracula* (1960) and *Countess Dracula* (1971).

The only three Dracula films in which Peter Cushing starred as Van Helsing alongside Christopher Lee's Dracula were *Dracula* (1958), *Dracula AD 1972* (1972) and *The Satanic Rites of Dracula* (1973). Cushing did, however, play Van Helsing in one other Dracula-titled film, and that was *The Brides of Dracula* (1960). He went on to play Van Helsing one last time in Hammer's final vampire movie, *The Legend of the Seven Golden Vampires* (1974). In this movie, Lee was conspicuous by his absence, as John Forbes-Robertson played Dracula.

Dracula Prince of Darkness was the only movie in which Lee did not utter a single word of dialogue as the evil Count. The story goes that when Lee read the lines he was supposed to say, such as "I am the apocalypse!" he totally refused to abide by the studio's instructions, deeming these lines "ridiculous".

In *Taste The Blood of Dracula*, the studio's original plan was to create a new Hammer star in the form of the young up-and-coming actor Ralph Bates. Apparently, at first, Lee refused to do anymore Dracula films unless the story was true to Stoker's original novel. Thus the movie began shooting without Lee as Dracula. However, when international distributors became very vexed at the prospect of a new Dracula film without Lee in the role, Lee was eventually tempted back by the offer of more money. But an increase in salary wasn't the only reason, for according to Lee himself, once he was told by a Hammer boss that if he did not return as Dracula, he would put a lot of people out of work, he finally gave in, as he said that was the last thing he wanted on his conscience.

Vincent Price was originally cast to play one of the three distinguished but decadent English gentlemen who inadvertently revive Dracula at Lord Courtley's blood-drinking ritual in *Taste The Blood of Dracula*. However, due to budget cuts, the studio could not afford to pay Price, and so he was released from the contract.

Dracula Has Risen From The Grave is especially noted for its religious undertones. For example, as the main protagonist, Paul (Barry Andrews), is an atheist, he clashes with the devout beliefs of his girlfriend's father, Monsieur Muller (Rupert Davies), who admonishes him at the dinner table for denying the existence of God. In addition, when

Paul is called upon to stake Dracula in his coffin, he is urged by the accompanying priest to pray over the vampire's writhing form, as faith is also essential to the complete destruction of the count. As Paul is unable to do so due to his being an atheist, Dracula is able to extract the stake from his chest with little difficulty.

Dracula Prince of Darkness was written into a novel by John Burke as part of his 1967 book *The Second Hammer Horror Film Omnibus*.

Dracula Prince of Darkness was filmed back-to-back with *Rasputin, The Mad Monk*. The two movies used many of the same sets, props and cast, including Christopher Lee, Francis Matthews, Barbara Shelley and Suzanne Farmer.

Barbara Shelley had rather an unfortunate accident whilst filming *Dracula Prince of Darkness*: she swallowed one of her fangs and had to drink a glass of salt water (a familiar emetic) to bring it back up again due to both the tight shooting schedule and the lack of a spare set of fangs.

When Hammer's first *Dracula* (1958) movie was released on a special Blu Ray edition in 2012, lost footage of the count's destruction was restored from a badly damaged Japanese print.

The Dracula movie that sees Christopher Lee at his most sadistic is *Scars of Dracula* (1970). In this film, not only does Dracula bite his victims' necks in his usual bloodthirsty way, but he also brutally stabs to death one of his female residents, brands the bare back of his servant Klove with a red-hot iron, and horribly slaughters the main protagonist's brother, who was unfortunate enough to set foot inside the count's mountaintop castle.

Scars of Dracula is the movie where some elements of Bram Stoker's novel are restored. For example, we see Dracula crawling down the exterior walls of his castle like some loathsome human lizard, just as he did in the book. Dracula is also presented as a charming but sinister host, behaving very closely to the way he did in Stoker's classic novel. Also, Dracula does tend to talk more in this movie than he did in the previous Dracula films, reminiscent of the loquacious manner he presents to Jonathan Harker in the book.

Jenny Hanley's voice in *Scars of Dracula* was dubbed by a lady called Nikki Van der Zyl.

Scars of Dracula was the movie that finally broke the continuity story in the Hammer Dracula series. Although, at the end of the previous movie *Taste The Blood of Dracula*, Dracula met his demise in an old desanctified church in England, Scars opens with Dracula being resurrected by a blood-spewing bat back in his Transylvanian castle. No explanation is given as to just how his ashes arrived back in his native home.

Taste The Blood of Dracula's storyline has often been criticised for the way Dracula immediately vows revenge on the three men who killed his "servant" (Lord Courtley). Critics deem this "ridiculous", as for one thing, Dracula didn't even know Courtley, and for another, why would Dracula seek to punish those three men who were responsible for resurrecting him in the first place? On the contrary, these critics argue, the vampire should have been "patting them on the back" for giving him life again!

The Satanic Rites of Dracula, which was Lee's very last appearance as the count in a Hammer movie, has often been described as the "James Bond Dracula film", for it features similar aspects to those you'd often see in an 007 yarn, like action-packed car chases, secret societies and a diabolical plan to destroy the world with a deadly plague.

TV cameras covered the London premiere of *Dracula* in 1958.

Dracula AD 1972, like *Scars of Dracula*, again breaks continuity with the previous film, for it opens in 1872 with Dracula (mysteriously) battling Van Helsing on a runaway coach in London's Hyde Park. It also sets a new short series in the Dracula Hammer films, bringing Dracula into modern times and ending with *Satanic Rites of Dracula* in 1973.

The soundtrack of *Dracula AD 1972* was composed by Manfred Mann member Mike Vickers.

Dracula Has Risen From The Grave was the first Dracula film to be passed by the censors in Australia, the previous movies - *Dracula* (1958) and *Dracula Prince of Darkness* (1966) - having been banned.

Some scenes in *Taste The Blood of Dracula* were filmed in Highgate Cemetery, said to be the lair of the notorious Highgate Vampire. The (matte-painted) church in which

Alan Toner

Lord Courtley performed the blood rite leading to Dracula's resurrection was approached via a gated section of the cemetery called the Collumbarium.

In the two modern-day Dracula movies – *Dracula AD 1972* and *Satanic Rites of Dracula* – Van Helsing's granddaughter was played by two different actresses. In the former, she was played by Stephanie Beacham, and in the latter, she was played by Joanna Lumley.

Among the many talking books that the late, great Sir Christopher Lee has narrated, he has (well, naturally) done one on Bram Stoker's original Dracula novel.

In *Dracula Prince of Darkness*, Lee's stunt double, Eddie Powell, became trapped underwater during the drowning scene and very nearly died.

The cloak worn by Christopher Lee in the very first Hammer Dracula movie was discovered in 2007 in a London costume shop. Missing for 30 years, the garment is said to be valued at $50,000.

Christopher Lee often complained about the red contact lenses he had to wear when playing Dracula. He found them to be extremely uncomfortable and awkward to wear. They were also very hard to see through.

According to Christopher Lee, he was paid just £750 for his very first Dracula role. He also said that the movie eventually grossed 25 million dollars at the box office.

The Hammer Horror Fact Book

In *Dracula* (1958), Peter Cushing actually does the stunt where he leaps over the banister himself, contrary to the studio's concerns that he might cause himself an injury.

3. The Frankenstein Films

Peter Cushing played Baron Victor Frankenstein six times for Hammer. The movies, in chronological order, were: *The Curse of Frankenstein* (1957), *The Revenge of Frankenstein* (1958), *The Evil of Frankenstein* (1964), *Frankenstein Created Woman* (1967), *Frankenstein Must Be Destroyed* (1969) and *Frankenstein and The Monster From Hell* (1974).

To get Frankenstein's methods of surgery spot on, Peter Cushing would often study how doctors operated, where they cut when performing brain transplants etc. In doing this, it was his intention to convince any doctors who may be watching in the audience of his authenticity when portraying the scientist.

The only Hammer Frankenstein in which Cushing did not appear was *The Horror of Frankenstein* (1970), in which Ralph Bates played the evil scientist.

Peter Cushing was his most wicked and ruthless as Baron Frankenstein in *Frankenstein Must Be Destroyed* (1969). In fact, in this movie, many Hammer fans deemed the Baron as more of a monster than the actual monster itself!

The Evil of Frankenstein was the first in the Hammer

Frankenstein series to break continuity with the previous movie. Whereas in *Revenge of Frankenstein*, the Baron ends up assuming a new identity after having plastic surgery to repair his mutilated features, Evil starts off like an entirely new Frankenstein story, with the penniless Baron - who is much less evil in this movie than he was in the previous two - returning to his family castle to revive his monster, whom he stumbles upon frozen in ice.

In *Curse of Frankenstein*, Hammer could not use the original Karloff monster makeup due to copyright held by Universal, so they had to come up with their own take on the creature's physical appearance for Christopher Lee. However, as Evil of Frankenstein was distributed by Universal Pictures, Hammer was then free to copy elements from the Universal franchise. That is why the creature bears some resemblance to the square-headed Karloff version, and why a lot of the laboratory equipment is so reminiscent of that used in the old Universal Frankenstein movies.

During the title sequence of *Evil of Frankenstein*, Cushing's Baron, brow beaded with sweat from the exertion, is seen cutting vigorously away at a cabbage. The cabbage was used to simulate the crunching sound of slicing through bone, although this was eventually censored with the title music.

Frankenstein Created Woman is the first in the series that incorporates supernatural elements alongside the scientific. In this story, Baron Frankenstein experiments with the process of transferring an actual human soul into another human body - with disastrous results, of course.

Alan Toner

The lovely Veronica Carlson starred in two Frankenstein movies for Hammer: *Frankenstein Must Be Destroyed* (1969) and *Horror of Frankenstein* (1970).

David Prowse, who played the monster in both *Horror of Frankenstein* and *Frankenstein and the Monster from Hell*, was also famous for playing Darth Vader in *Star Wars*.

Prowse also has the distinction of being the only actor to have played the monster more than once in the Hammer Frankenstein series.

In *Frankenstein and the Monster From Hell*, real human blood was used in this film, according to actor Shane Briant, who played Simon. The story goes that blood that could no longer be used for transfusions was sourced from the blood bank for use in the movie.

Frankenstein and the Monster From Hell was the last film directed by Terence Fisher before his death on 18th June 1980 at the age of 76.

Peter Cushing is quoted as saying that the wig he wore in *Frankenstein and the Monster From Hell* made him look like Helen Hayes.

On the set of *The Curse of Frankenstein*, the long-time friendship between Christopher Lee and Peter Cushing was forged when Lee stormed into Cushing's dressing room and complained, "I've got no lines!" Cushing calmly responded, "You're lucky. I've read the script."

The Hammer Horror Fact Book

In between takes of *The Curse of Frankenstein* – and indeed on many other occasions throughout their friendship – Lee and Cushing would often amuse themselves by exchanging "Looney Tunes" phrases (e.g. Lee would imitate the voice of Sylvester the Cat, which would often send Cushing into complete hysterics).

It has often been said by film historians that Hammer's *Curse of Frankenstein* was the movie that really revitalised the horror genre, which had been on a steady decline since its heyday of the Universal horror films of the 1930s and 1940s.

The original concept for *Curse of Frankenstein* was a black-and-white production, with Boris Karloff reprising his role as the Monster. However, Universal threatened to sue Hammer if this project went ahead. Therefore, Jimmy Sangster was forced to scrap this script and redo the story, bringing in Christopher Lee to play the Monster and Jack Asher to shoot the movie in Eastman colour.

In *Curse of Frankenstein*, the painting on the staircase shown to Professor Bernstein by Baron Frankenstein is Rembrandt's 1632 work "The Anatomy Lesson of Dr Nicholaes Tulp" Much like the evil Baron's own actions, the painting depicts the dissection of a hanged criminal, namely Aris Kindt.

Originally, Carry On star Bernard Bresslaw was considered for the part of the monster in *Curse of Frankenstein* on account of his height.

Alan Toner

Australian actor Kiwi Kingston played the part of the monster in *The Evil of Frankenstein* (1964).

In *Frankenstein Must Be Destroyed*, Peter Cushing deplored the rape scene, and even took his co-star Veronica Carlson out to dinner to discuss it. Putting her at her ease, he assured her that the Baron's attack on the terrified Maria was "not him", and that she should bear that in mind during the scene.

This controversial rape scene was actually added at the last minute, after shooting was nearly done, as the head of Hammer Studios, James Carreras, thought the film lacked "sex".

When *Frankenstein Must Be Destroyed* was released in Spain, it was limited, and only in the subtitled version.

The Revenge of Frankenstein (1958) was originally going to be titled Blood of Frankenstein.

Revenge of Frankenstein was Michael Ripper's first horror film for Hammer, although prior to that he did appear in a couple of non-horror productions for the studio.

In America, *Revenge of Frankenstein* was released as a double bill with *Night of the Demon*.

The German-born actress, Susan Denberg, who played the woman brought back to life in *Frankenstein Created Woman*, was also a Playboy centrefold model.

The Hammer Horror Fact Book

In *Frankenstein Created Woman*, Susan Denberg's voice is dubbed by Nikki Van der Zyl.

4. Werewolves, Reptiles and Zombies

Curse of the Werewolf (1961) was the only werewolf movie made by Hammer.

In *Curse of the Werewolf*, the interior of the inn where Leon is staying is the same interior featured in Dracula's castle in *Dracula* (1958).

The makeup artist who worked on Oliver Reed in *Curse of the Werewolf*, Roy Ashton, took the inspiration for his makeup from Jack Pierce's makeup from *The Wolfman* (1941).

In the original screenplay of *Curse of the Werewolf*, the beggar character was initially supposed to be a werewolf/rapist. However, due to problems with the censors, Hammer had to write this out.

Curse of the Werewolf is based on the novel *The Werewolf of Paris* by Guy Endore.

Curse of the Werewolf is set in 18th Century Spain.

Curse of the Werewolf was adapted into a 15-page comic

strip for the January 1978 issue of the magazine *House of Hammer*.

In *The Reptile* (1966), makeup artist Joe Ashton used appliances created from a mold taken of real snakeskin.

Star of *The Reptile* Jacqueline Pearce was well known for suffering claustrophobia, which is why she hated having to wear the reptile makeup in the movie.

The Reptile was filmed back-to-back with *The Plague of the Zombies* (1966), reusing many of the same sets, including the main village set on the backlot at Bray studios.

The Reptile was the last film of George Woodbridge.

A novelization of *The Reptile* was written by John Burke as part of his 1967 book *The Second Hammer Horror Film Omnibus*.

The cottage used in *The Reptile* was situated in Brentmoor Road, Woking, Surrey.

The Reptile is set in the same 19th century Cornish setting as the same year's *Plague of the Zombies*.

A high definition transfer of *The Reptile* was released by Studiocanal on Blu Ray and DVD as part of their ongoing restoration of Hammer's movie library.

Plague of the Zombies was filmed back-to-back with The Reptile, using many of the same sets.

Alan Toner

Plague of the Zombies was released as a double feature with *Dracula Prince of Darkness*.

A novelization of *Plague of the Zombies* was written by John Burke as part of his 1967 book *The Second Hammer Horror Film Omnibus*.

John Carson, who played the malevolent Squire Clive Hamilton in *Plague of the Zombies*, also starred in two more movies for Hammer, which were *Taste The Blood of Dracula* (1970) and *Captain Kronos: Vampire Hunter* (1974).

5. The Mummy Films

The Mummy (1959) was the first film made after Hammer reached an official agreement with Universal, which allowed them to do remakes of Universal's classic films. For example, in *The Mummy*, the agreement with Universal allowed Hammer to use the name "Kharis".

The original graphic scenes of Kharis getting his tongue cut out were removed for the British censor. The shotgun death was also trimmed.

A glass fibre replica of a sarcophagus, specially created for *The Mummy* movie, exists in the collection of the Perth Museum and Art Gallery.

Peter Cushing said that he suggested the scene in *The Mummy* where he drives a spear through the mummy. He claims he was inspired by the pre-release poster depicting the mummy with a shaft of light passing through it.

Although Hammer originally intended *The Mummy* to be a remake of the Karloff 1932 Mummy movie, the film's plot and most of its main characters were taken from Universal's *The Mummy's Hand* (1940) and *The Mummy's Tomb* (1942). The climax of *The Mummy's Ghost* (1944) was also included in the movie's plot, although with a different outcome.

Hammer made a total of four Mummy movies: *The Mummy* (1959), *The Curse of the Mummy's Tomb* (1964), *The Mummy's Shroud* (1967), and *Blood From The Mummy's Tomb* (1971).

Blood From The Mummy's Tomb, starring the lovely Valerie Leon as a reincarnated Egyptian princess, was a modern take on Bram Stoker's novel Jewel of the Seven Stars.

Ingmar Bergman is said to have had a copy of *Blood From The Mummy's Tomb* in his movie collection.

In *Blood From The Mummy's Tomb*, Andrew Keir replaced Peter Cushing after one day's shooting, as Cushing had to leave the set to care for his ailing wife.

In *The Curse of the Mummy's Tomb*, Franz Reizenstein's theme from Hammer's original *The Mummy* is audible during the Egyptian flashback scenes.

The Curse of the Mummy's Tomb was released as a double feature with The Gorgon (1964).

The Mummy's Shroud is based on a story and screenplay by British screenwriters Anthony Hinds and John Gilling.

Eddie Powell, who plays the mummy in *The Mummy's Shroud*, was also a stuntman in future films. He often doubled for Christopher Lee in the Dracula movies.

Although Peter Cushing was thought to be the unknown narrator of *The Mummy's Shroud*, this work was actually done by a guy called Tim Turner.

The Mummy's Shroud was the last Hammer movie to be shot at Bray Studios.

The screenplay for *The Mummy's Shroud* was written in just five days by John Gilling and Anthony Hinds.

The Mummy's Shroud was adapted into a 12-page comic strip for the December 1977 issue of *House of Hammer* magazine.

David Buck was originally the second choice for Paul Preston.

The design used for the mummy's face in *The Mummy's Shroud* was based on an actual one exhibited in the British Museum.

Whilst filming *The Mummy*, Christopher Lee sustained a series of injuries to his body, including a dislocated shoulder and injuries to his knees and shins.

Wanting to create the impression that the tomb in *The Mummy* hadn't been unearthed for thousands of years, the director of photography, Jack Asher, got a crew member to climb into the catwalks above the set and spray the air with water before the start of each scene. As the water particles descended, they would take all the smoke and dust with

Alan Toner

them, leaving the air completely clear.

6. The Quatermass Films

Hammer made a total of three Quatermass movies: *The Quatermass Xperiment* (1955), *Quatermass II* (1957) and *Quatermass and the Pit* (1967).

Professor Bernard Quatermass was a fictional scientist created by writer Nigel Kneale for BBC TV.

The Quatermass Xperiment (1955) was Hammer's highest grossing film up to that time.

The Quatermass Xperiment was released under the title *The Creeping Unknown* in the USA.

The Quatermass Xperiment was based on the 1953 BBC TV series *The Quatermass Xperiment*.

Nigel Kneale did have some reservations about Hammer's adaptation of his story. For instance, he took a dim view of the use of American actors Brian Donlevy and Margia Dean. Kneale also hated Les Bowie's tripe-based realisation of the monster. Kneale was further enraged by the BBC's decision to deny him any involvement or payment for his work. This was because as a contracted staff member, all rights were exclusive to the Corporation and not the individual.

Alan Toner

The reason for the "Xperiment" spelling in *The Quatermass Xperiment* was that Hammer wanted to exploit the fact that the British Board of Film Censors had instituted the use of the "X" certificate in 1951 to denote that certain films had subject matter that might be too explicit for persons under the age of 16. This movie was the first X-rated British SF movie, so Hammer availed itself of this honour by using "X" in the film's title.

Paul McCartney's ex-girlfriend, Jane Asher, played the little girl trying her ignorant best to befriend a transmogrifying Victor Carroon. Shades of *Frankenstein* (1931) here, where little Maria and Frankenstein's Monster meet up.

In *The Quatermass Xperiment*, Les Bowie used tripe and bovine entrails to enhance the monster's appearance.

The Quatermass Xperiment garnered something of a notorious reputation for itself Stateside. In 1956 the parents of Stewart Cohen tried to sue the Lake Theatre and distributors United Artists for negligence after their nine-year-old son died of a ruptured artery in the cinema lobby at a double showing of this movie with *The Black Sheep*. Consequently, Cohen carved a name for himself in *The Guinness Book of Records* as the only known case of someone literally dying of fright whilst watching a horror movie.

Quatermass II (1957) was released as Enemy From Space in the United States.

Just like it predecessor, *Quatermass II* was based on the

BBC TV series *Quatermass II*.

In *Quatermass II*, Brian Donlevy reprised his role as Professor Bernard Quatermass, much to the disapproval of Nigel Kneale, who had strongly criticised Donlevy's portrayal of the eponymous scientist in the first film.

Although it did quite well at the box office, the success of *Quatermass II* was greatly overshadowed by that of *The Curse of Frankenstein*, which was also released in May 1957.

Quatermass II was adapted into a 15-page comic strip for the August 1978 of the magazine *Hammer's Halls of Horror*. The strip was titled *Enemy From Space*.

In between takes of *Quatermass II*, Brian Donlevy's toupee was accidentally blown off by the aeroplane engine wind machines used during the movie's climax.

Quatermass II would be the last Hammer sequel to use a number in the title until *Woman In Black 2: Angel of Death*.

The wrecked town of Winnerden Flats featured in *Quatermass II* is at Ivinghoe Beacon, near the village of Ivinghoe, Buckinghamshire, and is owned by the National Trust.

Hammer originally wanted its sequel to *The Quatermass Xperiment* (1955) to be the Jimmy Sangster-penned *X The Unknown* (1956). However, Nigel Kneale prevented the use of his characters by another writer, which necessitated script revisions.

John Rae (McLeod) is the only actor in *Quatermass II* to reprise his role from the original TV series.

Quatermass and the Pit (1967) was a sequel to the two earlier Hammer Quatermass movies. Also, like its two predecessors, the movie was based on the BBC TV series *Quatermass and the Pit*, written by Nigel Kneale.

In the US, *Quatermass and the Pit* was released under the title *Five Million Years to Earth in March* 1968.

The DVD Region 1 release of *Quatermass and the Pit* from Anchor Bay includes a commentary by Nigel Kneale and Roy Ward Baker, as well as trailers and an instalment of a documentary titled *The Worlds of Hammer*, which focused on Hammer's Sci Fi movies.

A UK Blu Ray release of *Quatermass and the Pit* was released on 10th October 2011, followed by releases in Germany, Italy and Australia.

In *Quatermass and the Pit*, if you look more closely at the posters on the walls of the London Underground station, you will notice a few posters from other Hammer horror films, like *Dracula Prince of Darkness*, *The Reptile* and *The Witches*.

Andrew Keir celebrated his 41st birthday on the set of *Quatermass and the Pit* on 3rd April 1967.

The Hammer Horror Fact Book

Andre Morell was asked to reprise his role as Professor Bernard Quatermass from *Quatermass and the Pit*, but declined the opportunity.

Originally, Anthony Quayle was considered for the role of Professor Bernard Quatermass in *Quatermass and the Pit*, but it was Andrew Keir who was eventually cast.

In *Quatermass and the Pit*, when the workmen discover the skull during excavation, in reality they would have been bound by the law that says all further work should be halted whenever a relic or fossil is unearthed on any construction site.

During the late 1990s, there was talk that "The Crow" director Alex Proyas was planning a reboot of the *Quatermass and the Pit* movie, but this never came to fruition.

Andrew Keir did reprise his role as the Professor three decades later in "The Quatermass Memoirs", a five-part drama, scripted by Nigel Kneale, and broadcast on BBC Radio 3 in March 1996.

Quatermass and the Pit was the only movie in the Quatermass trilogy that Nigel Kneale actually liked. This was probably due to the fact that he was much more satisfied with Andrew Keir's performance as the title character than he had been with Brian Donlevy's in the previous two movies.

The script of *Quatermass and the Pit* is largely faithful to the

Alan Toner

original TV series.

A UK Blu Ray edition of *Quatermass and the Pit* was released on 10th October 2011, followed by releases in Italy, Australia and Germany.

The Anchor Bay Region 1 release of *Quatermass and the Pit* features a commentary from Nigel Kneale and Roy Ward Baker, in addition to trailers and an episode of the documentary *Worlds of Hammer*, which focused on Hammer's sci-fi movies.

7. The Swashbuckling Films

Hammer made a total of four swashbuckling movies: *The Devil-Ship Pirates* (1964), *The Pirates of Blood River* (1962), *The Scarlet Blade* (1963), and *Captain Kronos - Vampire Hunter* (1974).

Christopher Lee starred in only two of the Hammer swashbucklers: *The Devil-Ship Pirates* and *The Pirates of Blood River*.

Screenwriter Jimmy Sangster likened the plot of *The Devil-Ship Pirates* to that of *The Desperate Hours* (1955), in which a gang of crooks holds a family hostage.

The naval battle that occurs in the opening of *The Devil-Ship Pirates* purported to be a re-enactment of a battle involving The Spanish Armada in 1588.

According to Jimmy Sangster, *The Devil-Ship Pirates* premiered in the United States before it did in Britain.

Christopher Lee said that during the making of *The Devil-Ship Pirates*, he was "badly bashed about." During the final, extremely tough, sword fight, he sustained quite a few cuts to his body, and was "bleeding all over the place."

Alan Toner

The Devil-Ship Pirates was released as a double-bill in the UK with *The Secret Seven* (1963).

The Devil-Ship Pirates takes place in August 1588.

In *The Pirates of Blood River*, according to Christopher Lee, the pond at Black Park was a horrible experience. Not only was the water polluted, but also the bottom consisted of several feet of mud, sludge, broken trees, branches and general filth. Then there were the mishaps: Michael Ripper nearly drowned, Oliver Reed contracted an ear and eye infection, and Lee claimed he couldn't even walk upstairs for nearly six months due to the after effects.

Sammy Davis Jr., a BIG Hammer fan, visited the set of *The Pirates of Blood River* during filming.

As the studio couldn't afford an actual ship to use in *The Pirates of Blood River*, the ship seen from a long shot in the beginning was actually a stock shot.

On its release, *The Pirates of Blood River* was initially given an 'X' certificate. However, this was eventually changed to a 'U' certificate by Hammer after some rather explicit scenes (e.g. Maggie's death by piranhas) were cut.

The Scarlet Blade was set during the English Civil War.

The Scarlet Blade was Hammer's 100th film.

The Scarlet Blade has been described as "the poor man's Robin Hood" by critics.

The Hammer Horror Fact Book

Captain Kronos, Vampire Hunter was the second and last film that Caroline Munro made under her Hammer contract after *Dracula AD 1972*.

Hammer initially planned to make a series of Captain Kronos films. However, due to poor box office receipts for the first Kronos movie, this plan was shelved.

Although *Captain Kronos* was filmed in 1972, it was not actually released until 1974.

The writer of *Captain Kronos*, Brian Clemens, originally had Simon Oates in mind for the part of Captain Kronos.

In *Captain Kronos*, Horst Janson's thick German accent was deemed much to thick for people to understand it, so Julian Holloway was brought in to loop his entire performance.

A novelization of *Captain Kronos*, written by Guy Adams, was released under the title Kronos and published by Arrow Publishing, in association with Hammer and the Random House Group, in 2011.

The popular 70s magazine *The House of Hammer* published a three-part strip of *Captain Kronos* from October 1976 to January 1977.

8. The Karnstein Trilogy

The three vampire movies in Hammer's Karnstein trilogy were: *The Vampire Lovers* (1970), *Lust For A Vampire* (1971) and *Twins of Evil* (1971).

Hammer did plan a fourth film in the Karnstein saga, which was to be titled either *Vampire Virgins* or *Vampire Hunters*. However, these plans never came to fruition beyond the fourth draft of the script.

The 1974 film *Captain Kronos - Vampire Hunter* does feature a female vampire who is also a member of the Karnstein family, so this movie is often considered to be part of the same continuity.

The vampires in Hammer's Karnstein movies differ from the conventional vampires like Dracula in that they can walk around in daylight and be totally immune to fire. Some of these characteristics are duplicated in *Vampire Circus* (1972).

The Vampire Lovers was based on Sheridan Le Fanu's 1872 novella *Carmilla*. This was one of the very early works of vampire fiction.

The Hammer Horror Fact Book

While filming *The Vampire Lovers*, Ingrid Pitt and the rest of the female cast members had difficulty getting through the scenes without bursting into giggles. One of the funniest incidents involved Ingrid's vampire teeth, which kept falling out and into Kate O'Mara's cleavage. This little mishap necessitated Ingrid having to steal some gum from one of the stage crew to stick the fangs back in.

The Motion Picture Association of America gave *The Vampire Lovers* an R rating due to the vampire bites inflicted on the women's bosoms.

The Vampire Lovers takes place in the year 1790.

Ingrid Pitt rejected the lead role in *Lust For A Vampire* because she thought the script was awful.

Ralph Bates claimed that his part in *Lust For A Vampire* was his least favourite performance.

Despite the fact that he was a very popular radio DJ, Mike Raven's voice in *Lust For A Vampire* was dubbed by Valentine Dyall.

In *Lust For A Vampire*, Jimmy Sangster replaced Terence Fisher at very short notice.

Peter Cushing was originally cast as Giles Barton in *Lust For A Vampire*, but left the set to care for his seriously ailing wife Helen. He was replaced by Ralph Bates.

Twins of Evil used the same set as the one used in *Vampire*

Alan Toner

Circus.

Twins of Evil was released as a double bill with *Hands of the Ripper* (1971).

Whilst playing his small cameo part in *Twins of Evil*, Dennis Price was in bad health and suffering great pain.

The two females who played the "Twins of Evil" - Mary Collinson and Madeline Collinson - were from Malta, and as their accents were too thick, Hammer dubbed their voices with British performers.

The Collinson sisters, who played the "Twins of Evil" were also Playboy models.

Of the three movies in the Karnstein trilogy, *Twins of Evil* has the least resemblance to the novel, as it adds a bewitching quality to the vampire element of the story.

The original cut of *Twins of Evil* included a short scene, which was edited out, in which the evil twin approaches her uncle. This scene appears incongruous to the general scenario, as their uncle is preoccupied with burning the other sister. Somehow, she teleports back home, and the wicked twin gives him a show.

British horror writer Shaun Hutson wrote a novelization of *Twins of Evil* in 2011.

Twins of Evil was adapted into an 18-page comic strip for the January-February 1977 edition of *House of Hammer*

The Hammer Horror Fact Book

magazine.

9. Rasputin The Mad Monk

Christopher Lee actually met Prince Yusupov and Grand Duke Dmitri Pavlovich, the assassins of the Russian monk Rasputin. He didn't do this as research for his later film role as *Rasputin The Mad Monk*, but met them when he was just as a child in the 1920s.

Christopher Lee also met Rasputin's daughter, Maria, in 1976. She told him that Lee had her father's "expression".

Rasputin The Mad Monk was filmed back-to-back with *Dracula, Prince of Darkness*, using most of the same cast members and sets.

Christopher Lee and Francis Matthews spent several days filming an extended fight scene for the movie's ending. However, most of this scene ended up on the cutting room floor, leaving Matthews's bleeding lip in the penultimate shot unexplained.

Hammer made sure to release *Rasputin The Mad Monk* with the disclaimer that this film was made for sheer "entertainment" purposes and, as such, should not be taken as historical accuracy set in stone. They took this precaution because MGM was sued in 1933 by Princess Irina Romanoff Yusupov, who claimed that an earlier film about Rasputin

The Hammer Horror Fact Book

had libelled her by erroneously depicting her as a mistress.

The small hut where Rasputin has a confrontation with the angry villagers was the same one that Charles and Diana Kent took refuge in *Dracula, Prince of Darkness*.

Rasputin The Mad Monk was released as a double feature in the USA with *The Reptile* (1966).

The movie emphasised Rasputin's terrifying powers of magic and his seduction of women. A good analogy here would be that of the other part that Lee played for Hammer so brilliantly: Count Dracula.

The original ending of the movie had the lifeless Rasputin lying on the ice with his hands held up to his forehead in benediction. However, it was considered too controversial for religious reasons, and so was removed. Stills of the original ending still exist.

The real-life Rasputin was poisoned, shot, stabbed, and finally thrown into the river where he drowned. The amount of poison slowed his system, so he didn't bleed out, so this is why other methods of violence were used to finally kill him.

Notwithstanding the lack of historical accuracy, *Rasputin The Mad Monk* works outstandingly well due to its combination of magic and realism, turning the tale of the infamous Russian mystic and womaniser into a typical roller-coaster-ride of an enjoyable, and quite original, Hammer horror film.

10. The Prehistoric Films

Hammer made a total of four prehistoric films: *One Million Years B.C.* (1966), *Slave Girls* (1967), *When Dinosaurs Ruled The Earth* (1970), and *Creatures The World Forgot* (1971).

One Million Miles B.C. is actually a remake of the Hal Roach movie *One Million B.C.* (1940).

The enduring iconic image of Hammer's *One Million Years B.C.* is the one depicting Raquel Welch, who played pretty cave girl Loana, clad in her skimpy, furry bikini. This image also became a bestselling poster.

Raquel Welch's voice grunting in *One Million Years B.C.* was dubbed by Nikki Van der Zyl.

Robert Brown, who played cave man Akhoba in *One Million Years B.C.*, wears makeup much similar to that worn by Lon Chaney Jr. in *The Cave Dwellers* (1940).

One Million Years B.C. was heavily promoted as Hammer's 100th production.

A poster of Raquel Welch in her skimpy prehistoric attire was featured in *The Shawshank Redemption* (1994).

The Hammer Horror Fact Book

Ursula Andress was originally considered for the part of Loana in *One Million Years B.C.*, but declined due to salary demands.

When the Shell people are attacked by the giant turtle in *One Million Years B.C.*, they refer to the creature as "Achelon". This is the actual scientific name for the animal.

Like the original movie, *One Million Years B.C.* was largely ahistorical, for it depicts dinosaurs and humans existing in the same period in time.

Most of the dinosaur figures used in *One Million Years B.C.* still exist.

One Million Years B.C. was adapted for a 15-page comic strip for the May 1978 issue of *House of Hammer* magazine.

One Million Years B.C. was released on Blu Ray on February 14th, 2017, by Kino Lorber Studio Classics. This included interviews with Raquel Welch and Martine Beswick, archival interviews with Ray Harryhausen, and other extra material.

The exterior scenes of *One Million Years B.C.* were filmed on Lanzarote and Tenerife in the Canary Islands, right in the middle of winter.

Slave Girls (1967) was released as *Prehistoric Women in America*.

Alan Toner

Slave Girls is often considered the weakest – and most ridiculous – movie in the Hammer prehistoric quartet, especially due to its far-fetched script. Moreover, it cheaply re-uses sets and costumes from left over from *One Million Years B.C.* It was shot in just four weeks due to budgetary restraints.

Despite the general failings of *Slave Girls*, Martine Beswick (who also starred in Hammer's *Dr. Jekyll and Sister Hyde*) delivers an excellent performance as the imperious Queen Kari.

Slave Girls was originally set to be the 'A' feature on a double bill with *The Old Dark House* (1963), but after Hammer boss James Carreras deemed it not up to the studio's usual standards, it was edited down from its original 91-minute length and released as a support feature on a double-bill with *The Devil Rides Out* (1968).

When Dinosaurs Ruled The Earth was essentially a remake of *One Million Years B.C.*

When Dinosaurs Ruled The Earth was filmed at Shepperton Studios and on location at Fuertaventura in the Canary Islands, between November 1968 and January 1969.

Because Ray Harryhausen was busy in America doing stop-motion work for *The Valley of Gwangi*, the animation of the dinosaurs in *When Dinosaurs Ruled The Earth* was done by Jim Danforth. In a clever marketing tactic, Warner had both movies released as a double bill.

The Hammer Horror Fact Book

A special 27-word caveman language was used for *When Dinosaurs Ruled The Earth*.

The original nude scenes filmed for *When Dinosaurs Ruled The Earth* were restored for release on home video.

Patrick Allen (Kingsor) also provided the opening narration for *When Dinosaurs Ruled The Earth*.

Originally, *When Dinosaurs Ruled The Earth* was supposed to include a T-Rex, but the creature was eventually cut out, as a rather conservative Hammer boss deemed its stance feigned the stereotypical stance of homosexual males.

The title of *The Creatures The World Forgot* is rather misleading, for it raises expectations of dinosaurs when in fact the movie is devoid of such creatures and instead centres on another tale of rivalry and conflict between dark-haired and fair-haired tribes.

On the set of *The Creatures The World Forgot*, Julie Ege had just given birth and so was feeling rather poorly, so she retired to bed early during the shoot. Consequently, the crew wrongly thought she was stuck up and contrived to keep her out of shoot as much as possible, much to the annoyance of Hammer.

Scant dialogue is spoken by the cavemen in *The Creatures The World Forgot*, apart from a few grunts and gestures.

All of the exterior scenes in *The Creatures The World*

Alan Toner

Forgot were shot in Namibia and South Africa.

The Creatures The World Forgot was released in the UK on 18th April 1971.

11. The Hands of the Ripper

The Hands of the Ripper (1971) features a storyline about Jack The Ripper's daughter, who emulates his murderous activities.

The movie was released as a double bill with *Twins of Evil* (1971).

After *Room To Let* (1950), this was the second Hammer film that featured Jack The Ripper as its main subject.

The American censors removed 16 seconds from the murder sequences.

For the climactic scenes in St. Paul's Cathedral, permission was requested and turned down to film on location. A replica was built instead.

This was the last film of Marjorie Rhodes.

Dora Bryan received a 'special guest star' credit.

The movie was directed by Peter Sasdy.

Lynda Baron's character is named after one of the Ripper's actual victims: Elizabeth Stride.

Alan Toner

The movie used the large Baker Street set at Pinewood Studios, which was left over from *The Private Life of Sherlock Holmes*, made the previous year.

12. The Anniversary and The Nanny

The Nanny was released in the UK on 7th November 1965, and in the US it was released on 27th October 1965.

Initially, the role of *The Nanny* was offered to Greer Garson, but she later declined, saying it would be bad for her career.

According to Hammer writer Marcus Hearn, Davis unsuccessfully tried to seduce the producer of *The Nanny*, Jimmy Sangster.

The Nanny was the last Hammer film to be made in black and white.

The 10-year-old co-star of *The Nanny*, William Dix, could not attend the movie's British premiere on account of the 'X' rating it earned.

The Nanny was the last film of Nora Gordon.

The director of *The Nanny*, Seth Holt, found Bette Davis "impossible" to work with.

Alan Toner

According to Hammer expert Marcus Hearn, Bette Davis again tried to unsuccessfully seduce Jimmy Sangster on the set of *The Anniversary*.

After try-outs at Brighton's Theatre Royal, the original play of *The Anniversary* opened at London's Duke of York Theatre in 1966.

Shooting of *The Anniversary* began on 3rd May 1967. After work on 8th May, Davis complained about Rakoff using television techniques to mark out the actors' moves and demanded that he be replaced. She then refused to show up for work the next two days, causing immense resentment among the cast, who sided with Rakoff because they liked him. As a result of her difficult actions, not only did Davis cost the production six days of unusable footage, but she also made it come to a complete standstill for two days.

The original director of *The Anniversary*, Alvin Rakoff, was eventually replaced by Roy Ward Baker, at the insistence of Bette Davis.

Whilst making *The Anniversary*, Bette Davis was required to wear self-adhesive eye patches for her part. These patches not only irritated her constantly, but they also affected her equilibrium.

The Anniversary was shot at Elstree Studios in Hertfordshire.

In its review of *The Anniversary*, one top TV magazine

described Davis as being "great" in her role, but that the film itself suffered from the "staginess" of the play on which it was based.

The original stage play of *The Anniversary*, written by Bill MacIlwraith, was first produced in the West End, with Mona Washbourne as Mrs Taggart.

The Anniversary received a West End revival in 2005, with Sheila Hancock in the title role.

13. Hammer House of Horror TV Series

The *Hammer House of Horror* TV series was first shown on British Television, on Saturday evenings, in the autumn of 1980.

The much-loved Hammer stalwart Peter Cushing returned to appear in one episode of the series, namely The Silent Scream, in which he plays a former Nazi concentration camp guard who is ruthlessly intent on continuing his experiments on human victims whilst under the guise of an apparently inoffensive pet shop owner.

The *Hammer House of Horror* TV series is to be released on Blu Ray in October 2017 by Network.

Each self-contained episode of the series featured a different kind of horror, from werewolves to witches, from ghosts to devil worshippers. The episodes were directed by Peter Sasdy, Alan Gibson and Tom Clegg.

The children's party scene in the episode 'The House That Bled To Death' was placed at No. 50 in Channel Four's 100 Scariest Moments show.

The Hammer Horror Fact Book

The 13 episodes of Hammer House of Horror are as follows: "Witching Time", "The Thirteenth Reunion", "Rude Awakening", "Growing Pains", "The House That Bled To Death", "Charlie Boy", "The Silent Scream", "Children of the Full Moon", "Carpathian Eagle", "Guardian of the Abyss", "Visitor From The Grave", "The Two Faces of Evil", and "The Mark of Satan".

There were plans to do another series of *Hammer House of Horror*, but much to the disappointment of Hammer fans, these plans never came to fruition.

Terence Fisher was due to direct an episode, but sadly died during pre-production.

The series was filmed in Wykehurst Place, Bolney, West Sussex.

14. The She Films

Hammer made two She films: *She* (1965) and *The Vengeance of She* (1968).

She was based on the novel by H. Rider Haggard.

Ursula Andress played the part of Ayesha in *She*.

Although the studio was satisfied with Ursula Andress's physical appearance in *She*, they found her Swiss German accent somewhat off-putting, so they had her voice dubbed by actress Nikki van der Zyl.

She was released in the UK on 18th April 1965.

To bring a touch of authenticity to their roles in *She*, Peter Cushing and Bernard Cribbins spent a day at Chessington Zoo learning to ride camels. They bonded over this and their shared interest of bird watching.

The voice of Andre Morrell in She was dubbed by George Pastell.

In 1958, Roger Corman announced that he would film *She* in Australia.

The Hammer Horror Fact Book

She was directed by Robert Day.

Originally, *The Vengeance of She* was planned to be a direct sequel to She. However, the script was rewritten at the last minute, and so the story went in an entirely different direction to its predecessor, replacing an immortal woman with an immortal man.

The Working title of *Vengeance of She* was *She - Goddess of Love*.

When Ursula Andress's contract with Hammer expired, she refused to appear in the sequel to She, so newcomer Olga Schoberova was cast in the title role instead.

Unlike *She*, *Vengeance of She* was very poorly received, both commercially and critically.

15. The Abominable Snowman

The Abominable Snowman (1957) was Peter Cushing's second Hammer film of 22. His first was *The Curse of Frankenstein* (1957).

The original title of *The Abominable Snowman* was *The Snow Creature*, but this was later changed when it was realised that another movie existed with the exact same title.

Just like the Hammer Quatermass films, *The Abominable Snowman* was based on one of Nigel Kneale's TV dramas: *The Creature* (1955).

In America, *The Abominable Snowman* was released as a double feature with *The Trollenberg Terror*.

In November 2013, plans were announced by Hammer to remake *The Abominable Snowman*, in the light of the success of Let Me In and The Woman In Black.

16. Countess Dracula

Countess Dracula (1971) was based on the true story of the Hungarian Countess Elizabeth Bathory, who lived from 1560 to 1614. Bathory was notorious for torturing and slaughtering young virgins, in whose blood she would bathe to preserve her youthful beauty.

Countess Bathory is credited for influencing our contemporary concept of Dracula as an entity constantly craving human blood for eternal youth and vitality.

Ingrid Pitt's voice was dubbed in *Countess Dracula*. This infuriated Pitt so much that she vowed never to speak to Peter Sasdy ever again.

Countess Dracula was shot on Pinewood sets originally built for *Anne of a Thousand Days*.

Countess Dracula was produced by Alexander Paal and directed by Peter Sasdy.

Diana Rigg was originally considered for the role of Countess Dracula, but when she turned it down, it was given to Ingrid Pitt.

The picture visible behind the opening credits is an 1896

Alan Toner

painting by Hungarian artist Istvan Cosk. It depicts the real Countess Bathory revelling in the torture of naked young women by her servants.

Synapse released a Blu Ray/DVD combo pack of *Countess Dracula* in the US in 2014.

Countess Dracula was released as a double bill with Vampire Circus.

17. The Hound of the Baskervilles

The Hound of the Baskervilles (1959) is based on the novel by Sir Arthur Conan Doyle.

It was the first movie adaptation of Doyle's story to be filmed in colour.

Peter Cushing stars as Sherlock Holmes and Christopher Lee stars as Sir Henry Baskerville. Andre Morell plays Dr Watson.

The movie was directed by Terence Fisher.

Filming took place at Chobham Common and Frensham Ponds, both in Surrey.

Cushing would later reprise the role of the ace sleuth in the BBC Sherlock Holmes series nine years later.

Cushing was actually a great aficionado of Sherlock Holmes, and brought his knowledge to the filming of the movie. For example, he suggested that the mantelpiece feature Holmes' correspondence transfixed to it with a jack-knife, as in the original stories.

Alan Toner

In the novel of Hound of the Baskervilles, the hound is given a rather demonic appearance through the use of phosphorus paint, but in the movie the same effect is accomplished with a mask. A brindled Great Dane played the hound.

The Hound of the Baskervilles was very well received by critics. Time Out described it as the "best Sherlock Holmes movie ever made, and one of Hammer's finest."

The movie was released in the UK on 4th May 1959.

Christopher Lee openly admitted he had a spider phobia, so the look of sheer terror on his face during the tarantula scene was probably genuine.

The Baskerville Hall set is a redress of that used for Castle Dracula in *Dracula* (1958).

Christopher Lee himself also went on to play Sherlock Holmes in a couple of movies, including two TV films in the 1990s.

The hound used in the movie was a real dog called Colonel. On the set before the hound launches its attack on Sir Henry Baskerville, they could not get Colonel to jump on Lee, so they resorted to "prodding" him into action. Lee gave up, but then, suddenly, Colonel lunged on him and bit right through one of his arms.

Because Peter Cushing did not like smoking the traditional

The Hammer Horror Fact Book

pipe used by Holmes, he kept a glass of milk close at end to alleviate the taste.

As a change from the rather lovable buffoon that Nigel Bruce played in the old Sherlock Holmes movies, Andre Morell was the first to portray Dr Watson as a more than competent assistant of Holmes.

In the original novel, there is no attempt on Sir Henry's life in the hotel, unlike in the Hammer movie.

In June 2015, Arrow Video released a special Blu Ray edition of the *Hound of the Baskervilles*, packed with all kinds of interesting features, including a 1986 documentary *The Many Faces of Sherlock Holmes* hosted by Christopher Lee.

18. The Devil Rides Out

The Devil Rides Out (1968) was based on the 1934 novel by Dennis Wheatley.

This movie presents Christopher Lee in one his rare "good guy" roles, as he plays the Duc de Richleau, who fearlessly and resolutely battles the evil forces.

The movie is set in 1930s London and the South of England.

Christopher Lee has often described *The Devil Rides Out* as his favourite film.

Although known for his keen interest in occult books, at the same time Lee has strongly emphasised in interviews that it is highly dangerous to meddle around with such satanic instruments as Ouija boards and black magic rites.

Hammer decided to do a film on a Dennis Wheatley novel because Christopher Lee, a great admirer of Wheatley's work, was very keen for them to do so.

The character of Mocata (Charles Gray) was actually based on Aleister Crowley in the original novel. Dennis Wheatley invited him to dinner for research purposes.

The Hammer Horror Fact Book

Hammer originally wanted actor Gert Frobe for the part of Mocata.

Patrick Allen did the voiceover for this movie.

For the American market, the movie's title was changed to *The Devil's Bride* because its original title made it sound too much like a Western.

The Devil Rides Out was released as a double feature with *Slave Girls* (1967).

The movie was filmed in Black Park Country Park, Wexham and Buckinghamshire.

Top fantasy author Richard Matheson wrote the screenplay for *The Devil Rides Out*.

The Devil Rides Out was released in the UK on 20th July 1968.

19. The Journey To The Unknown TV Series

Journey To The Unknown was a British anthology TV series produced by Hammer films, airing on UK screens in 1969.

With its fantasy and supernatural themes, the series was somewhat reminiscent of the American TV series *The Twilight Zone*.

The series ran for just one season, with 17 episodes.

The 17 episodes were: "Eve", "Jane Brown's Body", "The Indian Spirit Guide", "Miss Belle", "Paper Dolls", "The New People", "One On An Island", "Matikitas Is Coming", "Girl Of My Dreams", "Somewhere In A Crowd", "Do Me A Favour And Kill Me", "The Beckoning Fair One", "The Last Visitor", "Poor Butterfly", "Stranger In The Family", "The Madison Equation", and "The Killing Bottle".

The series had a very eerie and memorable whistling theme, composed by Harry Robinson of Hammer Films, in addition to a creepy title sequence featuring a roller coaster filmed at night at a deserted amusement park (which was actually Battersea Park Fun Fair).

The Hammer Horror Fact Book

Up to now, there has never been an official DVD release of the *Journey To The Unknown* series.

20. Dr Jekyll and Sister Hyde

Martine Beswick, who played Sister Hyde in this 1971 movie, has said that her topless scenes were originally intended to show full-frontal nudity, but she fell out with director Roy Ward Baker over how much she wanted to actually show, so they didn't speak to each other for a whole week.

Dr Jekyll and Sister Hyde is the third of three Hammer adaptations of Robert Louis Stevenson's novella *The Strange Case of Dr Jekyll and Mr Hyde*. The other two movies are: *The Ugly Duckling* (1959) and *The Two Faces of Dr Jekyll* (1960).

Caroline Munro was offered the part of Sister Hyde, but declined because it involved some nudity.

Ralph Bates met his wife, Virginia Wetherell, on the set of this movie, as they prepared to shoot the scene in which Bates as Dr Jekyll kills the prostitute, played by Wetherell.

Dr Jekyll and Sister Hyde was released in the UK on 17th October 1971.

21. To The Devil A Daughter

To The Devil A Daughter was Christopher Lee's last movie for Hammer until *The Resident* (2011).

The scene where Christopher Lee's character appears naked was actually performed by his stunt double, Eddie Powell, who was filmed from above in order not to show his face.

Directors Ken Russell and Mike Hodges were approached to direct the film.

Olivia Newton John was considered for the role of Catherine.

The two male lead characters, Christopher Lee and Richard Widmark, both passed away at the same age of 93.

Star Richard Widmark soon realised that this movie was beset by production problems and had to be talked out of quitting.

The movie is based on the 1953 novel by Dennis Wheatley.

Dennis Wheatley passed away a year after the movie had first launched in theatres in 1976.

Alan Toner

To The Devil A Daughter was the second Dennis Wheatley story filmed by Hammer after The Devil Rides Out (1968).

The ending of *To The Devil A Daughter*, which shows Lee's character mysteriously disappearing after sustaining a bump on the head, has often been criticised as being very disappointing, corny and rushed.

Dennis Wheatley himself actually condemned the movie, describing it as bearing very little resemblance to his novel and "obscene".

The movie is one of the earliest Nastassja Kinski films.

Because he thought the original novel by Dennis Wheatley was so poor, screenwriter Christopher Wicking had no compunction about changing the story extensively.

Surprisingly, *To The Devil A Daughter* did quite well at the box office, especially in Europe. However, the movie's success was still not enough to save Hammer from the financial problems besetting them at that time.

On the DVD release of the movie, there is a 24-minute "making of" documentary that discusses the film and the demise of Hammer studios. It's called "To The Devil . . . The Death of Hammer."

The movie was released in the UK on 4th March 1976.

Kinski was 15 years old at the time of her first full frontal nude scene.

The Hammer Horror Fact Book

Christopher Lee's line, "It is not heresy . . . and I will not recant!" was sampled by heavy metal band White Zombie for the song "Super-Charger Heaven". The movie's title was also referenced by White Zombie in the song "Black Sunshine" ("To the Devil, a daughter comes . . .").

The movie's rather abrupt conclusion was not the actual ending, because in the original script Lee's Father Rayner recovers from the rock, thrown by John Verney, and attempts to pursue Verney and Catherine. He is then struck by a lightning bolt as he crosses the circle. Even though this alternative ending was filmed, there is no surviving footage, just a couple of monochrome stills, which are shown on the DVD.

22. Vampire Circus

Vampire Circus was released in the UK on 30th April 1972.

Laurence Payne was cast at the last minute, replacing Anton Rodgers, who dropped out due to illness.

Vampire Circus, according to many Hammer books, went over schedule, necessitating the omission of some key scenes.

The movie was shot in six weeks.

The movie was filmed at Pinewood Studios, Iver Heath, Buckinghamshire.

Vampire Circus is referenced in Bloodsucking Freaks (1976).

The movie was directed by Robert Young.

An updated novelization of *Vampire Circus*, by Toady author Mark Morris, was published in 2012.

The Synapse Blu Ray release of Vampire Circus contains, among its special features, a documentary entitled THE BLOODIEST SHOW ON EARTH: Making

The Hammer Horror Fact Book

Vampire Circus.

23. The Legend of the Seven Golden Vampires

Peter Cushing returned as Van Helsing, for the last time, in *Legend of the Seven Golden Vampires*.

The movie was released in the UK on 6th October 1974.

This is the only Hammer "Dracula" film not to feature his name in the title.

Although Christopher Lee was offered the role of Dracula, he declined after reading the script.

This was the first of two Hammer movies shot back-to-back in Hong Kong.

The movie takes place in Transylvania in 1804 and China in 1904.

John Forbes-Robertson was extremely annoyed on learning that his voice had been dubbed by David de Keyser.

The movie was directed by Roy Ward Baker and Chang Cheh.

The Hammer Horror Fact Book

The film was released with various titles in different locations, including *The Seven Brothers Meet Dracula* and *Dracula and the Seven Golden Vampires*.

The DVD from Anchor Bay features both the *Seven Brothers Meet Dracula* and the original uncut *Legend of the 7 Golden Vampires*. It also features a recording of Peter Cushing narrating the story of the film, accompanied by music and sound effects, which was released as an LP record when the movie premiered.

24. The Woman in Black

The Woman In Black is based on the 1983 novella by Susan Hill.

Harry Potter star Daniel Radcliffe played the main protagonist of the story, Arthur Kipps.

The movie was released in the UK on 10th February 2012.

The music boxes and mechanical toys in the nursery scenes were not created specifically for the film, but were actual antique toys from the period. They were loaned to the production by a collector.

The boy who plays Daniel Radcliffe's son is his real godson.

The location used for the fictional Nine Lives Causeway (leading to Eel Marsh Island) is Osea Island's tidal causeway situated at the estuary of Blackwater River in Essex. Due to tidal conditions, the cast and crew were restricted to only 4 hours of working time per day at that location.

The Woman In Black was Daniel Radcliffe's first movie after the Harry Potter franchise.

This movie was a remake of a British TV film from 1989

with the same title.

Daniel Radcliffe's real life girlfriend, Rosie Coker, who is a production assistant in the movie, appears as The Woman In Black, in the reveal "Asleep Behind The Desk" scene.

Because the original ending showed both Arthur and his son being killed by a train, it was deemed too depressing by the test audience, so an alternate "happy" ending was used instead, in which Arthur and his son are reunited with their wife/mother.

The Woman In Black has been adapted into a stage play by Stephen Mallatratt.

In 2014 a sequel to *The Woman In Black* was released, titled *The Woman In Black 2: Angel of Death*. This movie is set 40 years after the events of the first film.

25. The Quiet Ones

Although *The Quiet Ones* was filmed in 2012, it wasn't actually released until 2014.

The movie takes place in 1974.

The film is loosely based on "The Philip Experiment", a 1972 parapsychology experiment conducted in Toronto, Ontario, to determine whether subjects can communicate with fictionalised ghosts through expectations of human will.

26. Let Me In

Let Me In (2010) is a remake of the 2008 Swedish vampire film *Let The Right One In*.

The movie tells the story of a bullied 12-year-old boy, who develops a friendship with a female vampire child.

The story is based on the novel *Let The Right One In* by Swedish author John Ajvide Lindqvist.

Elias Koteas, who plays the police detective, also provides the voice of Owen's father, John.

The movie was written and directed by Matt Reeves.

According to Hammer Films Executive Producer Nigel Sinclair, interest in the project initially began in the middle of 2007, before the original *Let The Right One In* had screened for audiences.

When Hammer adapted the film, a few changes were made, such as moving the location from the Stockholm suburb of Blakeberg to a small new Mexican town.

In April 2010, Hammer Films and Dark Horse Comics produced a four-issue comic book series based on the movie. The series was titled Let Me In: Crossroads, and it was a prequel to the film.

The movie was set in the 1980s.

Reeves used Ronald Reagan's "Evil Empire" speech as an example of American thought during that period.

The word "vampire" is only said once in the movie.

The Morse code message spelled out at the end of the movie's official trailer spells out the words "Help Me".

The rubbish bag that Richard Jenkins wears over his head during the murder scenes was the actor's idea.

Director Matt Reeves modelled the physical appearance and personality of Abby (Chloe Grace Moretz) after seeing photos of a 12-year-old homeless girl taken by Mary Ellen Mark. Moretz said the sadness of her character was decided on her by her and Reeves after seeing the photo.

Despite being asked twice by Owen, Abby never reveals her real name.

27. Wake Wood

The plot of *Wake Wood* (2009) centres on the parents of a girl who was killed by a savage dog. Through means of a pagan ritual, the couple are granted the opportunity to spend three days with their deceased daughter.

Wake Wood was released in the UK on 25th March 2011.

The movie was the first theatrical release from Hammer Films in thirty years.

The reason why the movie was partly filmed in Sweden was because director David Keating loved the Swedish horror movie *Frostbite* (2006).

The movie marked the film debut of Ella Connolly and Aoife Meagher.

Wake Wood shares many similarities with *Pet Sematary* (1989), in that both movies involve bereaved parents who have a chance to bring their child back from the dead – with disastrous consequences.

Wake Wood was filmed in County Donegal, Ireland, and Osterlen, Scania, Sweden.

Alan Toner

A novelisation of *Wake Wood* was written by K. A. John and published by Hammer Books in association with Random House in 2011.

Wake Wood has also been compared to The Wicker Man due to its pagan overtones and sinister village community.

28. The Resident

The Resident (2011) tells the story of a young doctor who suspects she may not be alone in her new Brooklyn loft. Also, she finds that her landlord has formed a disturbing obsession with her.

Making *The Resident* was a kind of bittersweet experience for Christopher Lee. On a gloomy note, he tripped over a cable during production and sustained an injury to his back. On a happier note, he was also made a knight whilst working on the movie.

The Resident was Christopher Lee's first Hammer film since *To The Devil A Daughter* (1976), 35 years earlier. It was also his final Hammer film before his death on 7th June 2015, aged 93.

Both Christopher Lee and Lee Pace starred in the Middle Earth franchise. Lee played Saruman in the *Lord of the Rings* trilogy, and Pace played Thranduil in *The Hobbit* trilogy.

The movie was shot in New York City and New Mexico from 21st May to 11th July 2009.

Author's Note

If you enjoyed this book, you might like to read my other Hammer title, HAMMER HORROR REMEMBERED, which you can purchase in both Kindle and paperback formats by clicking on this link:

http://bit.ly/2rDvlLB

You can subscribe to my official Newsletter at:

http://bit.ly/2rDvlLB

Alan Toner
www.alantoner.com

Printed in Great Britain
by Amazon